Original title:
Dear Self,

Copyright © 2024 Book Fairy Publishing
All rights reserved.

Editor: Theodor Taimla
Author: Isabella Ilves
ISBN HARDBACK: 978-9916-759-24-0
ISBN PAPERBACK: 978-9916-759-25-7

Self-Portrait in Words

A canvas of thoughts, broad yet so precise
In each brushstroke of letters, a hidden splice
Crafting my image with ink as my hue
In every sentence, a self I construe

Line upon line, my essence unfolds
Whispers of dreams, of tales never told
In metaphors lost, my spirit retreats
Paper and pen, where my soul competes

Wandering Thoughts

Through fields of ideas, my mind will roam
Footsteps unseen in the vast unknown
Chasing specters of what might have been
In labyrinthine paths, I wander within

Fragments of starlight, whispers from dreams
Ripple through consciousness, like softened streams
Echoes of moons past, in twilight they blend
In thought's vast expanse, beginnings and end

An Inner Voyage

Within silent seas, my spirit sails free
No guiding stars, just the heart's decree
Navigating through shadows, light yet unseen
Charting unknown currents in realms serene

Songs of sirens, in whispers they weave
Mysteries of self, in fog they conceive
Each wave a question, each gust a sign
Voyages inward, exploring the divine

My Silent Echo

In the chambers of my mind,
Where shadows softly creep,
A silent echo binds,
My secrets, deep in sleep.

Whispers of forgotten dreams,
Dance on the misty air,
Reflection of moonbeams,
The silence they ensnare.

A song without a note,
A cry that has no sound,
In the silence, dreams float,
In echoes, I am found.

Traces of My Essence

In the starlit blaze,
I see my essence trace,
Echoes of bygone days,
In every shadowed space.

Footsteps lightly tread,
Paths I cannot see,
Memories gently spread,
Eternal parts of me.

In the breeze's gentle sigh,
In the twilight's gentle hush,
A fragment of my sky,
In every whispered rush.

Inner Symphony

A symphony inside,
Where chaos finds a tune,
In rhythm, fears subside,
Under the watchful moon.

Each note a step within,
A journey to the soul,
Where melodies begin,
And inner voices roll.

Strings of thoughts, they play,
In harmonies so sweet,
In music, night and day,
Inner peace, my heartbeat.

Verses of My Heart

In the pages of my heart,
Where ink is cast with care,
Stories find their start,
Emotions woven there.

Each verse a tale untold,
A whisper to the night,
With courage, love is bold,
In shadows, finding light.

In every gentle rhyme,
A heartbeat's steady thrum,
Through echoes lost in time,
My heart beats like a drum.

Emotional Topography

Mountains rise with all my fears,
Valleys sink in pools of tears,
Rivers flow in passionate streams,
Forests hold my quiet dreams.

Desert lands where hope is dry,
Oceans wave a heartfelt sigh,
Winds of change reshape the land,
Trails anew by steady hand.

Memoirs of Me

Pages turned from days gone past,
Echoes linger, shadows cast,
Moments stitched in memory's thread,
Whispers of what once was said.

Journeys walked on patterned ground,
Secrets lost and then refound,
Portraits hung of laughter bright,
Visions danced in soft moonlight.

Inner Constellations

Stars aligned in inner space,
Guide my thoughts with gentle grace,
Nebulas of dreams unfurl,
Galaxies of hopes swirl.

Planets orbit round my mind,
In their paths my truths I find,
Constellations light my way,
In the dark, bright maps display.

Silent Affirmations

Words unspoken, deep and true,
Echo softly, known by few,
In the stillness, strength observed,
In my core, resolve preserved.

Whispers carried on the breeze,
Soothe my soul, bring gentle ease,
Quiet nods to self-belief,
Silent affirmations' relief.

Inner Solace

Amid the rush of daily quest,
I find a place where heart finds rest.
In shadows cast by ancient trees,
A whispered calm, a gentle breeze.

The worries fade, the fears subside,
Where inner peace and strength abide.
With every breath, a deeper dive,
In solace found, the soul's alive.

Through whispered winds, the mind does clear,
A silent chant only I hear.
Within this space, a sacred hold,
Where stories of my soul unfold.

Intimate Reflections on Paper

In ink, the depth of dreams does spill,
The heart reveals what mind can't still.
Each written word, a tender sigh,
A dance of thoughts, a subtle high.

On pages worn by time's embrace,
I find the echoes of my place.
A sanctuary, written lines,
Unveiling truths in hidden signs.

Each letter holds a secret sound,
In written worlds, I'm gently found.
Between the spaces of each phrase,
My spirit roams in soft displays.

Reflections in Solitude

In silence deep, the echoes ring,
A solemn tune the heart does sing.
Alone, I find the strength to see,
The mirror of my soul set free.

The quiet night, a sacred friend,
Its darkened arms, a place to mend.
With every thought, a story spun,
Of battles fought and wisdom won.

In solitude, I learn to trust,
The whispered winds, the starry dust.
Through shadowed paths, my spirit roams,
In solitude, I find my home.

Letters to My Soul

Dear soul, I've written to you here,
In hopes you'll find my thoughts sincere.
Through ink and time, I bridge the gap,
Of dreams I've held within my lap.

In every stroke, a secret shared,
Of moments when my heart was bared.
A dialogue with inner grace,
A journey to a sacred place.

These letters hold my deepest fears,
My whispered hopes, my silent tears.
In written words, a bond is sewn,
A love letter to the soul I've known.

Letters to My Soul

In the quiet of midnight, thoughts flow
From a mind seeking truth, endlessly so
Pages colored with dreams of old
Stories of courage, silently told

Each letter a piece of an unseen whole
Binding fragments of a weary soul
Written in ink, emotions pour
Seeking the answers, yearning for more

Time's gentle brush, erases the scars
Guided by whispers, beneath distant stars
Memories linger, as shadows unfold
Burning like fire, but tenderly cold

Life's symphony plays, a song so sweet
In every struggle, a chance to meet
The depths of the heart, the spirit's plight
Letters to my soul, in the darkest night

Whispers to the Heart

Softly they come, in twilight's embrace
Echoes of dreams, gently they trace
Paths of light, and shadows of yore
Whispers to the heart, forevermore

In the silence, they murmur so sweet
Through joy and sorrow, in rhythmic beat
Hoping and yearning, to mend and start
Calling aloud, to the waiting heart

Fields of golden, under the moon's gaze
Memories linger, in a wistful haze
Songs unsung, and tales that impart
Whispers seep in, deep to the heart

Seek not the noise, but the gentle touch
Of love's soft voice, that means so much
In every note, a harmony parts
Whispers to the heart, with open hearts

Reflections in the Mirror

Gazing deeply, in the glassy truth
A visage of time, from age to youth
Each line a marker, of journeys taken
Reflections in the mirror, hearts awaken

Eyes that whisper, tales untold
A world within, in silence unfold
Images blur, with dreams' endeavor
Reflection whispers, gone but forever

A mosaic of moments, both lost and found
With laughter and tears, they astound
In the mirror's gaze, I see so clear
Fragmented echoes, drawing near

Life's canvas painted, in hues of night
Sorrows fade with the morning light
In every glance, a story's glimmer
Reflections in the mirror, they shimmer

Echoes of My Thoughts

In the stillness, they drift and weave
From mind's depths, they take their leave
Whispers of silence, breaking through ought
Resonating softly, echoes of my thoughts

Through time's veil, memories teased
Scenes of joy, and pains appeased
With every sigh, a chorus wrought
Gently they linger, echoes of my thoughts

Life's riddle twines, a puzzle grand
In contemplation, truths expand
From dawn to dusk, in circles caught
Endlessly returning, echoes of my thoughts

By day they follow, by night diffused
A ceaseless stream, never refused
In quiet moments, solace sought
Enduring reflections, echoes of my thoughts

Personal Revelations

In the silence of the night,
Whispers of the soul take flight.
Hidden truths begin to soar,
Yearning for the light once more.

Beneath the stars, my fears unfold,
Stories of both young and old.
A mirror shows what lies within,
Unveiling reasons for each sin.

Shadows dance upon the wall,
As echoes of the past do call.
Each secret, furrowed deep in time,
Woven into life's grand rhyme.

Candles flicker, cold winds blow,
Truths emerge from long ago.
By moonlight's soft and gentle swell,
I understand my own heart's spell.

With dawn's embrace, I am reborn,
Embracing truths I once did scorn.
Personal revelations found,
Set my spirit, free, unbound.

Inward Journey

A path uncharted lies within,
Where shadows of my thoughts begin.
Each step reveals a hidden part,
A journey deep into the heart.

Whispers of the mind do play,
Guiding me along the way.
Memories like leaves they fall,
Crafting the story of my call.

Oceans vast within my soul,
Waves of peace and gnawing toll.
Currents of my hopes and fears,
Flow through rivers made of tears.

Ancient echoes, soft and clear,
Whisper truths I long to hear.
In the quiet, still and deep,
Secrets dormant, now I keep.

An inward journey never ends,
With every turn, the soul extends.
In this labyrinth, I find,
A universe within my mind.

Truths Untold

In the chambers of the heart,
Lies the jewel from which we start.
Truths untold but not unseen,
Nestled in the spaces between.

Echoes of a silent creed,
Written in both word and deed.
Timeless whispers hold the key,
To unveil our destiny.

Beneath the surface, worlds converge,
Hopes and fears, they ever merge.
In the dance of night and day,
Fates align and truths convey.

Silent cries and hidden scars,
Lie beneath our morning stars.
In their shadows, we may find,
Echoes of a deeper mind.

Truths untold, like ancient songs,
Speak of where the soul belongs.
In their wisdom, old and wise,
The heart's purest dreams arise.

Heartfelt Epistles

Upon the parchment white and true,
I pen the thoughts I have of you.
Heartfelt epistles, tender, kind,
Bridges from the heart and mind.

Each word a vessel, pure and fine,
Carrying love through space and time.
Memories of moments shared,
Feelings deep beyond what's aired.

Ink of hope and touch of grace,
Filling voids that time can trace.
Letters hold a gentle plea,
Reaching out eternally.

Sentiments in lines do weave,
Echoes of the souls that grieve.
Yet within their tender flow,
Seeds of joy begin to grow.

In the silent night they fly,
Heartfelt epistles to the sky.
Messages of love unbound,
In their wings, solace found.

Secrets from Within

Whispers carried on the wind,
Secrets wrapped in silence,
Echoes of a time once known,
Lost in their defiance.

Shadows dance in hidden caves,
Murky tales they tell,
Veils of night obscure the light,
In depths where spirits dwell.

Through the mists, an ember glows,
Truth seeks its own revealing,
Heartbeats mirror secret's flow,
Moments deeply healing.

Cryptic songs and ancient rhymes,
Pass along the ages,
In a book with unseen lines,
Folded secret pages.

Dreams will light the hidden path,
Stars like gems will guide,
Seek within the silent thoughts,
Where true secrets bide.

Ink of My Heart

The ink flows from my open heart,
A story yet untold,
Words break free and take their flight,
Feelings uncontrolled.

Memories etched in endless black,
Emotions stained in blue,
Every beat a line to trace,
Every tear a hue.

Pages turn with whispered scenes,
Of joy, of loss, of love,
Verse by verse, my soul unweaves,
As stars watch from above.

In each stroke, a life unveiled,
Pulsing through the ages,
Every chapter, every tale,
Marks my boundless pages.

Poetry binds the fragments tight,
In a dance of prose and art,
Imprinted with the truest form,
The ink within my heart.

Inner Worlds

Beyond the gates of waking life,
Lies realms of thoughts profound,
Silent lands where dreams take flight,
Unseen and unbound.

Mountains rise of sheer resolve,
Oceans deep with care,
Mystic lakes of peace and calm,
Lands of love laid bare.

Cities built from fleeting glimpses,
Castles of desire,
Gardens lush with hope and wonder,
Pathways lit by fire.

Timeless journeys, endless visions,
Traverse the unseen trails,
Where the winds of thought are endless,
And every whisper sails.

In these inner worlds of mine,
Ephemeral and bright,
Lies the truth of who I am,
In the silence of the night.

Mind's Musings

In quiet moments, thoughts align,
Ideas gently weave,
Threads of wonder, bright and fine,
The musings which conceive.

Imagined realms and sacred dreams,
Thoughts that dare to soar,
Flowing like the endless streams,
Upon a distant shore.

Questions rise with every dawn,
Answers left to find,
Each new thought a stepping stone,
On pathways of the mind.

Marvel at the boundless scope,
Creation's pure delight,
Nourished by the seeds of hope,
That bloom within the light.

Mind's musings, a tranquil stream,
A dance of endless grace,
Guiding softly, like a dream,
In life's eternal chase.

A Dialogue Unheard

In whispered winds, your voice I seek,
The echoes lost, the silence speaks.
A dialogue unheard, so frail,
In shadows deep, our souls unveil.

The moonlight casts a silent plea,
A secret bond, just you and me.
In realms unseen, our spirits blend,
A dialogue unheard, we transcend.

For every star, a silent sigh,
The night embraces, you and I.
A dialogue unheard, hearts feel,
In whispered winds, our truths reveal.

Soliloquy of the Self

In quiet moments, thoughts unfold,
A soliloquy of the self, untold.
Whispers of dreams, the heart's own voice,
In stillness found, a silent rejoice.

The mirror speaks, a tale of time,
Reflections deep, in prose and rhyme.
A soliloquy of self, so clear,
In solitude, the soul draws near.

Each breath a verse, a whispered plea,
In silent bonds, the self set free.
A soliloquy of hope and grace,
In quiet moments, shadows chase.

Exploring My Depths

To fathom depths, I dive within,
Where shadows end and light begin.
Exploring dreams, the heart's own tides,
In silent realms, the soul abides.

A river's flow, the mind's own stream,
In whispered thoughts, the visions gleam.
Exploring depths, I journey free,
A seer's quest, in mystery.

The inner worlds, they call and sing,
With echoes vast, on spirit's wing.
Exploring depths, I come to find,
The boundless realms, of heart and mind.

Epistolary Reflections

In ink and paper, thoughts confessed,
Epistolary reflections, words caressed.
A written bond, through time and space,
In letters found, a soul's own grace.

The pen, it dances, heartfelt lines,
With whispers soft, the heart defines.
Epistolary dreams unfold,
In written words, our stories told.

Each letter sent, a piece of me,
Epistolary, wild and free.
A bond so strong, through ink we weave,
Reflections deep, in lines believe.

Epistolary Reflections

Ink stains on yellowed paper
Whispers of a distant past
Time has turned to vapor
Memories forever cast

Love letters never sent
Folded in a secret drawer
Moments of joy they've spent
Now shadows on the floor

Eyes that once met mine
Across the crowded room
Fleeting, yet divine
Vanished into gloom

Fragments of conversations
In corners of my mind
Lost in reflections
Of a life left behind

Epistolary echoes call
From pages worn and old
In the silence of it all
Their stories still unfold

Introspective Whispers

In the hush of twilight
Questions softly rise
Whispers of the night
Seeking no disguise

Glimmers of the past
Flicker, fade away
Moments spent too fast
In the light of day

Heart's quiet reflection
In silent, sacred space
Gently, with affection
Touches every trace

Dreams in shadows deep
Secrets held within
Inward, where they keep
Where my thoughts begin

Introspective whispers
Murmur through my soul
In their tender lispers
Find my spirit whole

Soul's Letters Unsealed

Unfolding the creases of time
On parchment thin as air
Each line a secret rhyme
Etched with tender care

Messages not spoken
But felt in every beat
Voices soft and unbroken
In the silent street

Through celestial ink
With stars as every dot
On the cosmic brink
Mysteries unforgot

Beneath the moonlit veil
Where shadows gently fade
Unseal the heart's mail
In twilight serenade

Soul's letters unsealed
In whispers of the night
Stories long concealed
Now dance in the light

Hushed Inspirations

In the stillness of dawn
Muses softly stir
Born with light first drawn
Without a single word

Thoughts like streams converge
To a river deep and wide
In the quiet they emerge
From the soul, inside

Hushed inspirations speak
In a language clear and true
From the places deep and meek
In dreams' soft velvet hue

Guided by whispers frail
Through realms of unseen grace
Inspiration's gentle trail
To a sacred place

Hushed, the inspirations flow
A chorus softly sung
In the heart's quiet glow
New verses are begun

Scenes from Within

In shadows cast by morning light,
Where whispers dance in silent flight,
A realm of dreams unfolds so tight,
In colors bright, yet out of sight.

Through corridors of thought, I roam,
Each step a pulse, each turn a home,
Inwards, towards a mind unknown,
Where seeds of mystery have grown.

A garden blooms with doubts and fears,
With vines that twist through hidden years,
Yet in this maze, sunlight appears,
To chase away those shadowed tears.

The heart beats deep, a constant hum,
A rhythmic song, both fierce and numb,
As scenes from within gently come,
Their tales unsung, yet never done.

In silence, echoes find their form,
In quiet, chaos can transform,
Within my soul, a curious storm,
Where thoughts in fervor overlap and swarm.

Witness to My Story

I've walked through paths both bright and drear,
Each step a mark through far and near,
As time unfolds, I see it clear,
The tale that's written year by year.

In moments past, the seeds were sown,
By hands unseen, yet not unknown,
A journey meant for me alone,
With every smile and every groan.

The years have sculpted valleys deep,
With memories that gently seep,
Into the soul where dreams do sleep,
In quiet waves, they rise and sweep.

The pages turn as heartbeats play,
A symphony in night and day,
The story's witness, come what may,
With words that dance and thoughts that sway.

In ink of life, the plot is drawn,
With hope anew at every dawn,
As witness to the dusk and dawn,
My story lives and carries on.

Chronicles of My Heart

Beneath the layers of my chest,
A story lives, a secret quest,
Of love and loss and dreams expressed,
In whispers soft, my heart confessed.

With every beat, a tale unfolds,
Of laughter bright and sorrows cold,
In chapters rich, both young and old,
A chronicle of truths retold.

In silent nights, the stars aglow,
Reflections of the heart's deep woe,
Yet in their light, new hopes can grow,
In endless tides, they ebb and flow.

For every tear, a lesson learned,
In every joy, a page has turned,
Through love's own fire, my spirit burned,
With fervent passion, unreturned.

Yet here I stand, with heart in hand,
A testament to moments grand,
The chronicles of love I've planned,
In every beat, anew they stand.

Inner Echoes

Within the hollow of my chest,
Echoes whisper, never rest,
Of thoughts unsaid and dreams confessed,
In quiet, they are manifest.

Each echo tells a story faint,
Of fears and hopes that dreams might paint,
In hues of joy and tears so quaint,
In silent art, they do acquaint.

Through labyrinths of mind, they weave,
With shadows cast and truths they leave,
In echoes soft, they interleave,
A tapestry that we can't perceive.

In every silence, echoes grow,
A symphony of inner glow,
Through hidden depths, they ebb and flow,
In undertones, their secrets show.

Yet though their whispers might be thin,
Their resonance is found within,
With echoes clear, they shall begin,
To speak the soul's unending hymn.

Personal Soliloquies

In quiet moments, thoughts unfold,
Stories whispered, softly told.
Alone with dreams, the heart converses,
Waltzing through life's hidden verses.

Reflections cast in evening's hue,
A mirror of the soul's own view.
Words unspoken, yet so clear,
In solitude, the truth is near.

Questions rise like morning mist,
Grasping moments, none are missed.
Pondering paths that lie ahead,
In solitude, no word is said.

Silent echoes, past interweaves,
With future hopes, the mind believes.
Woven threads of fate we see,
A personal soliloquy.

In twilight's grace, the spirit bends,
Conversing where the silence ends.
Night's embrace and dawn's first light,
Soliloquies through endless night.

Journey into Self

Embarking on a journey inward,
Past memories, where truths are savored.
Steps untaken, paths unknown,
In solitude, the self is grown.

Waves of thought in endless sea,
Seeking answers, where could they be?
Heartbeats drum an ancient tune,
Guided by the inner moon.

Far within, a world apart,
Secrets held within the heart.
Echoes of the days gone by,
In this journey, we rely.

Mountains scaled in silent mind,
Wisdom in what we find.
Valleys deep of joy and sorrow,
Mapping out the bold tomorrow.

Through the maze of inner space,
We find ourselves in time's embrace.
A journey into self we take,
With every step a new awake.

The road is long, yet we persist,
In seeking truth we can't resist.
Journey of the soul, so profound,
The self within, there to be found.

Silent Self-Talk

Beneath the whispers of the day,
Silent words with heart we say.
In the quiet, truths align,
In silent self-talk, thoughts entwine.

Mirrors of the soul reflect,
Echoes of the mind's dialect.
Intimate, this silent speech,
Within our core, the lessons teach.

Underneath the guise of calm,
Resting in a mental balm.
Conversations deep and wise,
In the silence, insights rise.

Boundless streams of thought traverse,
Quietly, the mind converses.
Solace found in hidden phrases,
Guiding through life's endless mazes.

Each unspoken syllable,
Holds a truth, invisible.
In silent self-talk, we confide,
The deepest thoughts, where truths reside.

Mindful Murmurs

In moments still, the whispers start,
Echoes murmured from the heart.
Mindful murmurs, soft and clear,
Guiding steps with gentle cheer.

Waves of thought in mindful streams,
Shaping hopes, defining dreams.
Cascades of calm, in silence flow,
In these murmurs, wisdom grows.

Silent ripples through the mind,
In their depths, the peace we find.
Mindful murmurs, secrets told,
In their grace, the heart's consoled.

Echoes soft of inner speech,
To the soul, these whispers reach.
Mindful of each fleeting word,
In their presence, truth is heard.

Calm descends, as whispers blend,
Infinite, the messages they send.
Mindful murmurs, guiding light,
Illuminating darkest night.

Within These Walls

Within these walls, the echoes bare
Of whispers lost in quiet air
A tapestry of hopes confined
In shadows where the dreams align

The weathered stones do secrets keep
In corners where the spirits seep
The silence hums its sacred tune
Beneath the watch of pallid moon

Through rusted gates, the stories pass
In reverent shadows they amass
The whispers dance on cobbled floor
Of lives and loves forever more

Within these walls, the heart does yearn
For days of light that might return
Yet in the hushed and hallowed halls
A timeless peace within these walls

The Unseen Me

In mirrors, I do seek my face
Yet find a world devoid of grace
The echoes of a silent plea
For someone to unveil the me

Enshrouded in a cloak of who?
The many masks I've crafted new
The fragile threads of self untwine
In shadows, where my truths resign

Invisible to every eye
The tears unnoticed as they dry
Behind the veil, a soul set free
The silent song, the unseen me

Between each breath, my essence lies
A symphony in hushed disguise
For in the depth of what can't be
Lies all the strength of the unseen me

Epistles of Existence

In letters bound by space and time
The whispers of existence rhyme
A dance of ink upon the page
To tell a tale, both young and sage

From dawn to dusk, the tales unfold
In epistles writ, the truths are told
Of joy and sorrow, love's embrace
The timeless etch of life's own grace

The ink, it carries hearts and souls
Through countless lives, it gently strolls
A script set free on feathered wings
To tell of all that being brings

Each letter holds a fragment true
Of every heart that beat and flew
The epistles of existence weave
A tapestry none can conceive

My Silent Inquiry

Beneath the vast and endless sky
The questions form, but voices shy
A whisper carried by the breeze
A silent query in the trees

The stars above, they wink and gleam
Awake within a hidden dream
Yet still the silence, like a shroud
Enfolds the thoughts I dare not loud

In twilight's grasp, the heart does seek
The answers buried, soft and meek
The quiet lays its gentle touch
On restless minds that ache too much

My silent inquiry breathes low
In shadows where the secrets grow
For though the world may hear them not
The heart will seek, and questions sought

Heartfelt Monologues

In the silence of my mind,
Thoughts like echoes intertwine.
Whispers of my heart confined,
In shadows where they softly shine.

Dreams of yesteryears gone by,
Ripple in the still night sky.
Hushed hopes that never die,
In this monologue, I can't deny.

Love like embers faintly glow,
In the quiet depths below.
Cradled in this tender flow,
Where secrets softly grow.

Time stands still, a gentle host,
Memories like fleeting ghosts.
In my heart, they linger most,
In whispered tales, almost.

Words unsaid, like morning mist,
Lost in moments, lightly kissed.
In this monologue, I'm gently kissed,
By dreams that still persist.

Inner Soliloquy

Beneath the stars, in twilight's hush,
A soliloquy begins to blush.
Silent whispers softly rush,
In the soul's sweetest hush.

Questions linger, answers fade,
In the shadows, light is laid.
Heartstrings gently played,
In thoughts that serenade.

Loneliness, a quiet friend,
In the silence, comforts lend.
In this soliloquy's blend,
Wounds begin to mend.

Hopes and fears, a woven thread,
In the space within my head.
In the quiet, softly said,
Dreams and dreads are spread.

In the depths of inner night,
Thoughts take gentle flight.
In this soliloquy's light,
I find a new insight.

Unwritten Confidences

In the journal of my heart,
Words unspoken softly start.
Whispers in the quiet part,
Where my confidences chart.

Fears and dreams in silent thread,
Woven thoughts inside my head.
In the quiet, softly read,
Pages of the unsaid.

Love like ink on paper flows,
In the hidden, gentle shows.
In this quiet prose,
My secret garden grows.

Hopes in lines yet to be,
In the pages' silent spree.
Unwritten, wild, and free,
Confidences that are me.

Heartfelt thoughts in shadows cast,
In the lines that softly last.
In this journal's silent past,
My confidences are amassed.

Personal Echoes

In the hallways of my mind,
Echoes of my heart you'll find.
Whispers in the silence bind,
Memories of a kinder kind.

Softly, gently, they return,
In the quiet, they still burn.
Lessons that I've yet to learn,
In echoes, I discern.

Lonely moments, tender scars,
Whispers of the distant stars.
In these echoes, no more bars,
Finding peace in old guitars.

Hopes and dreams in echoes play,
In the quiet, they relay.
In a soft and gentle way,
They brighten up my day.

Personal echoes softly call,
In the silence, not too small.
Within me, they gently fall,
In echoes, they enthral.

Fragments of My Mind

Pieces floating, thoughts adrift
In the silence, meanings shift
Wisps of dreams, unseen they twine
Echoes of a life, intertwined

Misty memories, scattered far
Chasing shadows, shifting stars
In the corners, truths reside
Hidden doors, just steps inside

Haunted whispers, ghosts that sing
Songs of solace, they softly bring
Threads of time, they intertwine
Fragments lost, yet still they shine

Fleeting moments, etched in sand
Marking paths where shadows stand
In the maze of thoughts confined
Journey deep, in fragments find

Coloring whispers, shades of night
In my mind, a silent flight
Words unspoken, left behind
In the fragments, thoughts unwind

Mind's Inner Libraries

Shelves of whispers, thoughts enshrined
Books of knowledge, meticulously aligned
Words like lanterns, softly glow
In the quiet, wisdom flows

Chronicled memories, pages turn
Lessons learned, old fires burn
Binding truths, in leather bound
In the silence, secrets found

Ink like rivers, thoughts cascade
In the margins, mysteries fade
Stories woven, lives entwined
In the library of my mind

Tomes of solace, grief and joy
Past and present both deploy
In each chapter, lives are sown
In these pages, I am known

Vast cathedral, silent roar
In this refuge, I explore
Libraries vast, thoughts defined
In the echoes, peace I find

Heart's Private Collection

Treasures hidden, locked away
In the heart, where shadows play
Moments cherished, softly kept
In the silence, they have wept

Photographs of days gone by
Laughter, tears beneath the sky
Memories in fragile frames
Whispered stories, silent names

Gentle mementos, tokens dear
Whispering tales for hearts to hear
Letters worn from yesteryears
In the heart, preserved from fears

In the vault, where love resides
Secrets rest, where peace abides
Bonds unbroken, time has spun
In this quiet, tears may run

Every heartbeat holds a key
To this rich complexity
In this haven, stories dwell
Heart's collection, stories tell

Introspective Diary

Pages turn, reflections speak
In this diary, secrets leak
Thoughts unspoken, ink reveals
Every feeling, deeply feels

Moments captured, day by day
Whispers written, fears allay
In the quiet, thoughts conspire
Written lines, hearts' desire

In each word, a soul laid bare
Hopes and dreams, a quiet prayer
Journals of a life unseen
In these pages, I am keen

Chronicles of joy and pain
Every loss, and every gain
In the margins, voices sing
Of the truths that shadows bring

Private musings, hidden deep
In this tome, my soul does keep
Introspections, intertwined
In this diary, thoughts confined

Moments of Clarity

In silence, truths unfold, dreams collide
Twilight whispers, time takes a side
Solitude births thought, undefined
In clarity, lost fears unwind

Soft dawn cradles, secrets revealed
In the hush, wounds tender, concealed
Epiphanies spark, briefly distilled
In clarity, the heart's dreams fulfilled

Doubt dissipates, shadows extinguish
In pure light, the soul's lustre distinguish
Moments of stillness, vision relished
In clarity, fears banished, diminished

Whispers of wisdom in the cool air
The chill of truth, laid bare, unaware
Night's dark curtain draws, moments rare
In clarity, pure, simple, no despair

Fleeting glimpses of crystalline thought
The essence of life, untangled, caught
In that pause, clarity is sought
In clarity, calm, peace life has brought

Discovering My Essence

Gently peeling layers, unveiling core
In whispers old, truth to explore
Seek within, soul's depths adore
In essence, unbound, forever more

As dusk fades softly, self untangled
In night's still embrace, light spangled
Mysteries whisper, mind unraveled
In essence, pure, spirit unshackled

In shadows' play, identity refined
Through the silent stir, heart aligned
Emerging strength in fears confined
In essence, pure, soul inclined

Rain's gentle touch, refreshes, renews
In the storm's breath, clarity ensues
Darkness fades, inner light imbues
In essence, found, life's hues

Striding forth, new dawn embraced
In self-discovery, truth faced
Boundless, free from fear laced
In essence realized, peace traced

Whispers of the Spirit

In the quiet, breath of winds still
Echoes faint, in the dawn's chill
Soft murmurs, spirit's will fulfill
In whispers, truth's gentle thrill

By the shore, waves speak low
Tales of old, where breezes go
Heart listens, in whispers flows
In spirit's breath, soul's glow

Among the trees, leaves confide
In hushed tones, where dreams reside
Barefoot paths, spirit as guide
In whispers, faith can't hide

Moonlight drapes the sky with grace
Night's calm voice, spirit's embrace
Truth revealed in that silent space
In whispers, spirit finds its place

In the silence, spirits intertwined
Harmony tracing hearts aligned
In divine whispers, peace is signed
In spirit's voice, solace find

Heartfelt Reflections

Quiet moments, heart's soft yearning
Twilight falls, candles burning
Reflections in time, love discerning
In heartfelt dreams, the soul's churning

Fleeting seconds, emotions collate
In whispers low, visions translate
Memories crafted in fate's slate
In heartfelt thoughts, love is innate

Gentle touch, hearts recombining
In each beat, love's subtle finding
Through reflection, life reassigning
In heartfelt sighs, hearts are binding

Silent dusk, universe communes
In twilight's breath, hope attunes
Love's reflections, in heart runes
In heartfelt songs, soul's tunes

Emotions flow, tides intertwine
In soft whispers, echoes align
Heartfelt musings, love's design
In reflection, the world shines

Whispers from Within

In the quiet of the night,
Whispers call from deep inside.
Echoes of my heart's delight,
Where my secret dreams abide.

Softly, they begin to speak,
Words so gentle, pure, and sweet.
Stories of the strong and weak,
Ancient tales they now repeat.

They remind me who I am,
Under layers, thick and thin.
Not the lion, nor the lamb,
But the fire held within.

So I listen, and I learn,
From these whispers, soft and true.
Feel their warmth, and let them burn,
Guiding me in all I do.

In the end, I understand,
These whispers are my own.
Like the shifting, golden sand,
They turn the unknown known.

Journey to Me

On a path that winds and turns,
Through the valleys, over streams,
Every lesson that I learn,
Leads me closer to my dreams.

With each step, the road reveals,
Mysteries of days gone past.
In each moment, time congeals,
Building truths that always last.

Mountains rise and rivers flow,
Nature's song, a guiding star.
In their rhythm, I know,
Who I am, both near and far.

In the mirror of the lakes,
See my soul, so wild, so free.
With each choice my spirit makes,
I'm on this journey to me.

Through the dark and through the light,
Every shadow, every beam.
I'll keep walking, day and night,
Toward the essence of my dream.

Inner Dialogues

Silent whispers fill my head,
Thoughts that dance and intertwine.
In these moments, softly said,
Truths and doubts, the thin line.

Voices that I can't dismiss,
Echoes from my very soul.
In their chorus, darkness, bliss,
Seek to make my spirit whole.

Questions turning, answers nigh,
Veiled in shadows, light attained.
Conversations in the sky,
From this dance, wisdom gained.

But the clash of thought and mind,
Forge a path that's truly mine.
In the dual, peace I find,
With each word, a clearer sign.

Inner dialogues, a stage,
Where my fears and hopes convene.
In the silence, from the rage,
I emerge, serene, unseen.

Epiphanies of the Heart

In the quiet, dawn's first light,
Feel a spark ignite my soul.
Epiphanies break the night,
Making fractured pieces whole.

Moments when the world aligns,
And the heart can truly see.
Unspoken dreams, hidden signs,
Share their sacred clarity.

Truths that only love reveals,
Gentle as a lover's kiss.
In these tender, quiet fields,
Find the meaning, find the bliss.

Every heartbeat, every breath,
Carries whispers of the wise.
In this dance of life and death,
See the world through knowing eyes.

Epiphanies of the heart,
Clear the fog, and light the way.
In their glow, a brand new start,
Guiding me through every day.

Pages from the Heart

In quiet rooms, the whispers play,
Of love and loss, night's tender sway.
On pages worn, the secrets keep,
Where heartbeats find their solace deep.

Ink traces dreams, emotions bare,
A story woven, rich and rare.
Beneath the moon, in pages' glow,
Heart's hidden truths begin to show.

The scent of time on paper's edge,
Memories bound in fragile pledge.
Each tear and smile, a chapter's mark,
The journey bright, the paths so dark.

In every line, a lover's plea,
A wishful breath, eternally.
Pages turn with soft caress,
Heartfelt whispers to confess.

Letters from the Soul

Beneath the stars, where twilight sings,
Soul's letters fly on silent wings.
To distant hearts, they find their way,
Through night and dawn, in light of day.

Unseen by eyes, yet felt so near,
Each word a tear, a joy, a fear.
In script unseen, emotions spill,
From soulful heart, their truths fulfill.

Between the lines, a story told,
Of love and sorrow, brave and bold.
Each letter sings a timeless tune,
Embraced by sun, caressed by moon.

In dreams they soar, on whispered breeze,
To touch a heart, to find it ease.
Soul's letters hold a world within,
Of every loss and every win.

Intimate Musings

In silent thoughts, where shadows play,
Intimate musings find their way.
Through mind's embrace and night's reveal,
The tender truths begin to feel.

Like whispers soft, in evening's glow,
They paint a world we'll never know.
Yet, in the heart, they softly tread,
With words unsaid and tears unshed.

Among the stars, these musings dance,
In fleeting glance and longing chance.
They weave a tale both sweet and deep,
In waking hours and in sleep.

Eclipsing doubt, they comfort near,
A gentle voice, so pure, so clear.
In musings soft, when night is still,
Intimate truths the heart fulfill.

Unmasking Me

In mirrors deep, a truth concealed,
The heart's own voice is then revealed.
Beneath the mask, the shadows flee,
To show the world, it's truly me.

In silent nights, where thoughts are free,
Unmasked, my soul begins to see.
The fear and doubt, they fade away,
As dawn brings forth a brighter day.

In echo's call, I find my name,
And with it, cast aside the shame.
To be oneself, the bravest quest,
A heart unmasked finds gentle rest.

In every scar, a battle won,
In every tear, the healing sun.
Unmasking me, the courage found,
In love's pure light, I'm truly crowned.

Whispers Through Time

In the silence of the night,
Ancient echoes softly chime,
Tales of love and loss ignite,
Whispers flowing through the time.

Stars above in silent dance,
Chronicles of days now past,
Moments lost in fleeting glance,
Memories forever cast.

Shadows lengthen, stories weave,
In the fabric of our minds,
Threads of life that we perceive,
In the whispers time unwinds.

Voices from the yesteryears,
Guide us through the veils of age,
Lessons learned through joys and tears,
Written on life's turning page.

Through the echoes, we find grace,
In each whisper, a sweet rhyme,
Carrying us through the space,
Timeless whispers, beyond time.

Dialogues Within

In the quiet of my mind,
Voices whisper, shadows speak,
Secrets in the silence find,
Depths of soul where thoughts do peek.

Questions weave through inner halls,
Echoes of the heart's refrain,
Searching through the mind's vast walls,
For the truths that still remain.

Whispers, murmurs, thoughts entwined,
In the caverns of my dreams,
Dialogues within, refined,
Speak in gently flowing streams.

Mind and heart in quiet talk,
Sharing mysteries profound,
In the soul's secluded walk,
Inner truths are gently found.

Dialogues in silent light,
Guide the spirit, calm the din,
In the stillness of the night,
Conversations flow within.

Conversations with My Essence

In the mirror of my soul,
There I see reflections gleam,
Truths and tales that keep me whole,
In the depths where dreams do stream.

Voices rise from heart's deep core,
Guidance in the silence heard,
Wisdom from the ancient store,
In each softly spoken word.

Through the echoes of my heart,
Conversations, gentle, flow,
Pieces of my self impart,
In the whispers, truth does show.

Dialogues with my inner being,
Light my path with insight's glow,
In the essence, clear and seeing,
Find the way, and gently grow.

Soul to soul, in silence, blend,
Boundaries fade, as spirits mend,
Conversations without end,
Essence to my essence, friend.

Heartfelt Musings

In the quiet of my heart,
Thoughts of you do softly bloom,
Feelings whisper, ne'er depart,
In the silent, tender room.

Memories on gentle wings,
Tales of moments, cherished, fly,
Heartfelt musings softly sing,
Echoes in the night's deep sky.

Love does weave its sacred spell,
In the stillness of the mind,
Heartfelt tales of us to tell,
In the musings, soft, we find.

Dreams and hopes in quiet play,
In the heart's most sacred space,
Thoughts of love that gently sway,
Heartfelt musings we embrace.

In the silence of our hearts,
Feelings flow in gentle streams,
Love's sweet song that ne'er departs,
Heartfelt musings in our dreams.

Introspection in Ink

Upon the page where thoughts do flow,
In inky swirls, where secrets grow.
Reflections deep, the soul's reveal,
Echoes of truths that time can't steal.

In silent words, the heart does speak,
A language hidden, rich and meek.
Emotions, raw, on parchment rest,
A silent journey, self-confessed.

Through rhythm's dance and stanzas grand,
We grasp to understand, withstand.
Each verse a mirror to the past,
Painting moments, held steadfast.

Ink bleeds into the fabric tight,
Of memory's quilt, both dark and light.
Unveiling layers, one by one,
An endless story, never done.

In solitude, with quill in hand,
The soul embarks, a promised land.
Tracing lines, where thoughts have been,
Introspection starts within.

Finding My Path

Wander upon life's winding way,
Through valleys deep, 'neath skies of gray.
A search for meaning, journey's quest,
In heart and mind, we seek what's best.

With every step, a lesson learned,
Through twists and turns, direction earned.
Trailblazing through the unknown wild,
With faith and hope, a humble child.

The world a canvas, vast and wide,
Each footprint left, a story's stride.
Across the terrain, highs and lows,
Emerging truth, life's ebb and flows.

Stars alight the path ahead,
While past decisions leave a thread.
In crossroads faced, we choose our fate,
And craft the lives we contemplate.

Beyond the doubts, horizons gleam,
A vision bright, a waking dream.
In finding self, through trials vast,
We shape our future from our past.

Soliloquy with Shadows

In twilight's hush where shadows play,
Whispering secrets, night and day.
A solitary voice, it sings,
Of hidden fears and unseen wings.

Shadows dance in muted sighs,
Reflecting truths and many lies.
In quietude, we converse deep,
With echoes of the past we keep.

Within the dark, we find the light,
Contrasting hues bring clarity bright.
The silent witnesses of time,
Compose a humble, peaceful rhyme.

A dialogue with forms obscure,
Of memories that still endure.
In shadow's realm, we find the grace,
Of our own shadowed, inner space.

This soliloquy, a sacred tune,
Beneath the watchful, patient moon.
In conversation with our shade,
Discover peace, where none invade.

Deep Within the Mirror

Reflections gaze from glassy lake,
Each thought a ripple, each breath a wake.
Beneath the surface, secrets lie,
In mirrored depths where truths comply.

Eyes that peer from silvered pane,
Show not just skin, but heart's domain.
A visage calm, emotions rage,
Deep within, an endless stage.

With every glance, a story told,
Of battles fought and dreams of old.
A silent witness, clear yet blurred,
Echoes of the soul's true word.

Transcend the sheen, to inner core,
Where shadows blend with light galore.
In seeking self, beyond the face,
We find compassion, love, and grace.

The mirror's depth, a boundless sea,
Reflecting all we strive to be.
Journey inward, past the guise,
To know the heart, beyond the eyes.

Messages Unspoken

In whispers of the twilight breeze,
Unseen truths find their release,
Between the stars and shadowed trees,
Silent voices never cease.

Eyes that meet in fleeting glance,
Languages of the heart, they dance,
Secrets held by circumstance,
In silent words, a grand romance.

Beneath the calm of night's domain,
Unheard whispers softly reign,
Songs of joy and silent pain,
In the quiet, we remain.

Veils of mystery intertwine,
In the hush, our souls align,
Unvoiced echoes through the pine,
In silence, meaning we define.

Between the edges of the known,
Messages unspoken, shown,
In the quiet, they have grown,
Silent words, a world of their own.

Embrace of Inner Wisdom

In the stillness of the dawn,
Where whispers of wisdom spawn,
Silent truths are gently drawn,
From within, a light reborn.

Pages turned within the mind,
Signposts of the past we find,
Guidance from the self, aligned,
In the silence, wisdom's kind.

Paths that twine through forests old,
Stories of the heart unfold,
In the quiet we behold,
Lessons precious, pure as gold.

Through the calm of evening's grace,
In our inner depths, we trace,
Truths that time cannot efface,
Wisdom's gentle, warm embrace.

From the depths of silent seas,
Comes a knowing, gentle breeze,
Inner wisdom sets us free,
Guides us to our destined peace.

Seeds of My Spirit

In the soil of dreams, I sow,
Seeds of spirit, hopes that grow,
With every sunrise, joy to show,
Life's garden thrives where breezes blow.

Roots of passion, deep they dive,
From the heart's core, power derived,
Through the storms that test and strive,
In resilience, they survive.

Blossoms of my soul take flight,
Petals kissed by morning light,
In their fragrance, dreams ignite,
With spirit's fire, bold and bright.

Gardens of the heart expand,
Nurtured by a loving hand,
In the spirit, seeds command,
Life's rich tapestry, so grand.

Through the seasons, growth I see,
In the spirit, wild and free,
Seed to blossom, destiny,
In nature's cycle, joyous plea.

Verses for Solitude

In the quiet of the night,
Where soft shadows hold the light,
Solitude begins its rite,
Words are gathered, taking flight.

Whispers of the mind unfold,
Silent stories, truths retold,
In the quiet, thoughts grow bold,
Verses formed in wisdom's hold.

Through the window, moonlight streams,
Casting light on whispered dreams,
In the calm, the spirit gleams,
Silent havens, peaceful seams.

In these moments, softly bright,
Solitude gives dear insight,
Words that flow as clear as night,
Verses paint the soul's delight.

Through the quiet, minds commune,
In their silent, heartfelt tune,
Solitude, a gentle boon,
Verses whispered to the moon.

Silent Contemplations

Beneath the stars, my worries flee,
Amid the night's serenity,
Quiet whispers in the trees,
Speak of dreams and mysteries.

Moonlit paths that wind and weave,
Through thoughts that no one else perceives,
Reflecting on life's gentle push,
In moments held in silent hush.

Waves that kiss the sandy shore,
Echo tales forevermore,
Silent hearts entwined by fate,
In whispers only night creates.

Wind that sings its ancient song,
Carries memories all along,
Silent contemplations, deep,
In dreamers' minds, where secrets sleep.

In the stillness, I find peace,
Every worry seems to cease,
Silent thoughts, like stars, align,
In this quiet heart of mine.

Pages of My Being

In the ink of memory traced,
Lives a story time won't erase,
Pages turned and gently worn,
By hands of fate, I'm gently torn.

Every line a breath, a spark,
Words that glow in deepest dark,
Chapters of a heart laid bare,
In swirling ink, I find my care.

Between the spaces, moments freeze,
Whispers caught in a gentle breeze,
Echoes of a softer time,
Pages flutter, rhythm and rhyme.

Truths and dreams on fragile leaves,
Bound in silence, none perceives,
Pages of my being hold,
Timeless truths in stories bold.

Through each word, my soul takes flight,
Transforming night into light,
Pages of a life unveiled,
In this book, my heart's detailed.

The Voice Inside

A whisper in the silent air,
Secrets that my heart would share,
A voice within, so soft, confined,
Speaking truths my mind can't find.

In quiet moments, bold and clear,
This inner voice, I hold so dear,
Echoes of my deepest dreams,
Guiding through uncertain streams.

When doubts and shadows cloud my sight,
This voice remains, a steadfast light,
Resonates within my core,
Urges me to seek and soar.

Through trials faced and tears untold,
The voice inside is strong and bold,
Holds me close, through darkest days,
Guiding me in graceful ways.

In every choice, in every stride,
List'ning to the voice inside,
Aligning heart with mind's design,
Knowing peace and strength are mine.

Heart's Quiet Reflections

In moments when the world is still,
My heart reflects, its voice is will,
Pondering life's gentle breeze,
Finding solace in the trees.

A quiet lake, a mirrored sky,
Reflecting dreams that softly lie,
In these ripples, thoughts unfold,
Stories in my heart retold.

Beneath the calm, a gentle hue,
Grateful whispers, old and new,
Heart's reflections, pure and bright,
Illuminating darkest night.

Embracing silence, I retreat,
Grounded by my own heartbeat,
Reflections that I come to trust,
Guiding me in ways so just.

Heart's quiet reflections sing,
In stillness, finding everything,
Within this peace, my spirit soars,
Forever seeking, evermore.

Unearthing Me

In quiet hours, the earth does speak,
Of secrets deep within its crust,
Whispers of lives that came to be,
In ancient voices, now turned to dust.

I dig with hands both trembling, sure,
To find the core of what was lost,
Layers peeled reveal the pure,
A self unearthed at endless cost.

Through roots and stones, truths long buried,
Surface in the light of day,
Fragments of a self once carried,
Pieced together, come what may.

Each shard, a story yet untold,
Of courage, fear, and fleeting time,
In the depths, a soul unfolds,
A song, a verse, a silent rhyme.

The earth within, both vast and small,
Bears the weight of you and me,
Ancient echoes, heed their call,
In unearthing, we set free.

Contours of My Being

Tracing lines on skin, unseen,
Contours of a world within,
Where dreams and fears convene,
In the silent dance of limb.

Beneath the surface, rivers flow,
Of memories both dark and light,
Through valleys deep where shadows grow,
And peaks that scale the endless night.

Mountains rise with every breath,
Each scar a testament to life,
The valleys echo love and death,
In heartbeats carved with timeless strife.

Eyes, windows to the soul's expanse,
Gaze upon the far and near,
In reflections, we find chance,
To see ourselves both blurred and clear.

Contours merge and contours part,
In the endless quest for being,
The map etched on each fragile heart,
Guides us through this life of seeing.

Journey Within

A path untraveled, silent, still,
Lies within the heart and mind,
A winding road, by sheer will,
To depths unseen, paths undefined.

Each step a revelation sweet,
Of hidden valleys, peaks unknown,
In the quiet, hearts do meet,
With truths that dare to be alone.

Through shadows cast by doubt and fear,
With lanterns forged in hope and time,
We journey inward, drawing near,
To the sacred and the prime.

Uncharted lands of thought and dream,
We traverse with bated breath,
In every soul, a hidden seam,
Where life ignites, defying death.

The voyage within, both gentle, fierce,
Leads us to the inner core,
In the mirror, we pierce,
The endless quest for evermore.

An Ode to My Being

In the quiet dawn, I find my grace
Between the night and day's embrace
Whispers of dreams softly create
A tale of love, a destined fate

Through shadows deep and skies so wide
I walk alone, yet none to hide
My spirit's strength, a guiding star
In paths unknown, both near and far

Mountains rise, they call my name
Echoes of my past, twin flames
I breathe the air, the earth, the sea
An ode to life, an ode to me

Mornings bloom with sunlit hues
In tender shades, my soul renews
The world may change, yet here I stand
A single note in nature's band

As daylight fades to twilight's wing
I close my eyes, my heart to sing
In every beat, in every tear
An ode to being, pure and clear

Intimate Revelations

In shadows deep, my secrets lie
Whispered truths beneath the sky
Intimate moments, softly shared
In passion's fire, so unprepared

Eyes that meet in silent gaze
Hearts that beat in tender maze
In words unsaid, a thousand dreams
Flow through us like celestial streams

The night unveils our hidden fears
Closeness melts away the years
Two souls entwined in quiet plea
Intimate revelations, you and me

Touch that speaks of ancient lore
Love that seeks forevermore
In every sigh, in every kiss
Moments of everlasting bliss

Dawn will break, and time will part
Yet we'll remain in heart to heart
For in this world, and far above
Intimate truths are bound by love

Unraveling My Core

Layers thick, and veils so fine
Hide the essence I define
In a maze of dreams, I journey through
Unraveling core, discovery new

Shadows dance, and walls confide
Secrets of my heart inside
With each step, a thread undone
A tapestry of battles won

In silent nights, where fears reside
I face the truth, I cannot hide
Within each tear, a story told
Unraveling core, brave and bold

In winds of change, I find my voice
Through trials hard, I make my choice
To live and love, to heal the pain
A spirit free, unbound by chain

The dawn breaks clear, a future bright
With newfound strength, I embrace the light
In every fiber, through and through
Unraveled core, reborn, renewed

Sacred Conversations

In twilight hours, whispers soft
Conversations, sacred, aloft
Spoken truths in hallowed night
Kindred souls in purest light

Words that bridge the vast unseen
In quiet moments, hearts convene
A being known, a trust so deep
Promises through silence keep

The cosmos listens to our plea
Sacred talks that set us free
With eyes that speak and hands that touch
In sacred bonds, we feel so much

In these hours, no masks to wear
Just genuine, beyond compare
A sanctuary, hearts align
Sacred thoughts in whispered line

The night will fade, but we return
Sacred lessons deeply learned
In every word, in every breath
Sacred conversations, beyond death

Chronicles of My Mind

In twilight's hush, my thoughts take flight,
Through labyrinths of day and night.
Whispers of memories, echoes that bind,
Weaving tales in the chronicles of my mind.

Dreams whisper softly in the quiet eve,
Luring with promises, as fantasies weave.
Midst shadows and light, truth I will find,
Hidden deep in the chronicles of my mind.

Lost in reverie, I wander and drift,
Seeking solace, through layers I sift.
Answers lie in the patterns they bind,
Woven tightly in the chronicles of my mind.

Moments of clarity, as stars pierce the dark,
Questions dissolve, leaving their arc.
Peace enfolds where once was confined,
Harmony reigns in the chronicles of my mind.

Inner Narratives

Voices within, a symphony play,
Each thread of thought, a part in the fray.
Coloring worlds with strokes so fine,
Dreams intertwine, my inner narratives shine.

Torments and joys, they both reside,
In chambers where shadows cannot hide.
Through quiet reflection, boldly I sign,
Life's winding path in my inner narrative line.

Wisdom and folly walk hand in hand,
Whispering secrets only I understand.
Through every emotion, boundaries define,
Crafting the tales of inner narratives in line.

Infinite worlds in the quiet I find,
Capture the essence of what is mine.
Each fleeting moment, inherently divine,
Spreads its wings in my inner narratives' design.

Soul's Musings

Under a canopy of celestial light,
The soul muses in the quiet of night.
Eternal questions, forever inclines,
Seeking answers in the soul's musings, combined.

Whispers of eternity, gentle and slight,
Guide footsteps through the darkest plight.
Journey of spirit, both weary and fine,
Records its path in the soul's musings refined.

Mysteries unfurl as dawn draws near,
Bringing whispers that only the soul can hear.
Infinite musings, graciously aligned,
Unveil their truth in the soul's musings enshrined.

In the dance of stars, reflections glisten,
To the heart's deepest yearnings, I listen.
Marking the passage where shadows resign,
Crystalline thoughts in the soul's musings entwine.

Intimate Letters Within

Scrolls of the heart, inked with pure light,
Unfold their tales in the deep of the night.
Cursive emotions on each line begin,
Whispered secrets in intimate letters within.

Love's gentle sighs, sorrows' tear stains,
Mark the parchment with joy and pains.
Unseen missives where true stories spin,
Revealed softly in intimate letters within.

Hope's golden threads, despair's dark hue,
Interlace moments that time both grew.
Memories linger where life had been,
Etched timelessly in intimate letters within.

Voices of yesteryears, softly they sing,
Melodies of life on tender wing.
Echoes of what is and what has been,
Eternalized in intimate letters within.

Whispers of My Heart

Softly, the echoes in silence start,
Their melodies drift like shadows apart.
A murmur sings in twilight's embrace,
Unspoken dreams in a silent space.

By moonlit paths my whispers tread,
Through night so deep, where fears are shed.
In shadows cast by brightest stars,
Lie secrets hid from day's cruel scars.

With every breath, a silent plea,
A yearning deep within the sea.
Of endless depths and boundless skies,
Where whispered hearts in silence sigh.

The whispering wind through meadows glide,
Carrying tales of love worldwide.
In every leaf, in each cool breeze,
Resides the heart's eternal ease.

Whispers grow as dawn ascends,
In a dance where sorrow mends.
And within the heart's pure art,
Lie eternal whispers from the start.

My Written Solace

In quiet moments, ink meets page,
A solace found within the cage.
Where thoughts like rivers freely flow,
In written words, my heart does know.

Each line a bridge to realms of peace,
Where aching souls find sweet release.
Through scribbled lines of pain and praise,
I navigate life's winding maze.

With pen in hand, I shape my dreams,
Crafting worlds amidst moonbeams.
Each verse a whisper, soft and clear,
My written solace drawing near.

In prose I find a silent grace,
A sanctuary's warm embrace.
The paper holds my deepest cries,
Reflecting truths that never die.

So, let my thoughts forever roam,
In written words I've found my home.
A solace forged in ink and light,
To soothe my soul through endless night.

Sentiments Inside

In the quiet corners of my mind,
Sentiments tender, intertwined.
Hidden truths in shadows dwell,
Whispered stories yet to tell.

Among the echoes of the past,
Sentiments rise and fall, steadfast.
In every heartbeat, every glance,
Lie fragments of a secret dance.

Through corridors of thought, they glide,
Sentiments I cannot hide.
Each moment etched in silent grace,
A timeless tale on memory's face.

In laughter's echo, in sorrow's tear,
The sentiments inside steer.
They weave a tapestry so grand,
Of who I am and where I stand.

Amidst the noise, they softly speak,
In every triumph, every peak.
In the stillness, they reside,
My soul's true voice, sentiments inside.

Stream of My Thoughts

Down winding paths my thoughts do flow,
Like rivers where soft breezes blow.
Through valleys deep and peaks so high,
They wander freely, touch the sky.

Each ripple carries dreams untold,
In streams where hopes and fears unfold.
They intertwine in endless dance,
A stream of thought, a fleeting trance.

With every whisper, every cry,
They drift beneath the endless sky.
A journey through the mind's expanse,
A flowing, ever-changing chance.

These thoughts like rivers carve their way,
Through night and dawn, through night and day.
In constant motion, never still,
A stream of thoughts, a wandering thrill.

And as they flow, they shape my soul,
In every part, within the whole.
A journey vast, a pathway broad,
Stream of my thoughts, where dreams are trod.

Past Self's Diaries

In ink-stained nights of yesteryears,
A voice from within softly appears.
Whispers of dreams once held so tight,
Unfold in the quiet of twilight.

Pages yellowed by time's embrace,
Reflect a heart once filled with grace.
Shadows of laughter, echoes of tears,
Mingle in diaries of forgotten fears.

Through scribbled lines of yore I see,
The essence of the past in me.
Fragments of hope and silent cries,
Woven beneath the evening skies.

Dreams deferred yet not erased,
In these pages, memories traced.
Each word a beacon to the past,
Diaries holding stories vast.

A journey through this time-bound maze,
Reveals the self in a tender gaze.
In diaries old, the heart still beats,
A bridge 'tween past and present feats.

Reflections on Paper

In moonlit glow, thoughts take flight,
On paper's stretch, they softly alight.
Silent whispers of a restless mind,
In each line, solace I find.

Ink flows like a river, serene,
Pouring out visions, felt but unseen.
Each word a mirror reflecting within,
Shadows of joy, whispers of sin.

Contours of a soul gently traced,
In fleeting moments, ideas embraced.
Pencil's grace, a silent guide,
As reflections in heart abide.

Glimpses of a life on paper bare,
Truths unspoken float in the air.
The dance of pen and parchment's kiss,
Creating worlds of silent bliss.

In written strands of thought's embrace,
I seek myself in this sacred space.
Reflections shimmering, clear and deep,
Secrets of my soul to keep.

Scribbles of My Soul

Between the margins of white and grey,
The scribbles of my soul hold sway.
Unfettered thoughts in chaos bloom,
In ink their beauty finds its room.

Each scribble a fragment of my mind,
In tangled lines, my heart defined.
Moments lived in strokes so wild,
My essence captured, unbeguiled.

Lines break free in frantic haste,
A dance of dreams and hopes misplaced.
From chaos, patterns start to form,
In scribbles, a quiet, sacred storm.

Ink-blushed fingers spell my truth,
In scribbles, the innocence of youth.
Resonance of a soul unchained,
In scattered marks my spirit gained.

Through spontaneity, I find my art,
In scribbles lies the beating heart.
Each curve and mark, a story told,
Whispers of my soul unfold.

Epiphany on Pages

In pages' fold, a light revealed,
Epiphanies once concealed.
Hidden truths like morning dew,
Unravel in a world anew.

Each line a spark of sudden grace,
Ideas birthed in silent space.
Thoughts entwined in paper's keep,
Awaken from their slumber deep.

Moments crystallized in prose,
Like petals of a blooming rose.
From ink's embrace, clarity springs,
The soul's epiphany it brings.

Journeys of introspective mind,
On paths through written words aligned.
In the quiet margin's expanse,
Wonders of life start to dance.

Pages whisper secrets old,
Epiphanies in stories told.
With each word, the heart unfolds,
In pages' grasp, the soul beholds.

Soft Whispered Realities

In the twilight where dreams collide,
Soft whispers echo, far and wide.
Unseen realms where mysteries bide,
Awaken gently, truth inside.

Silent whispers paint the night,
Hues of wonder, beams of light.
In soft shadows, hopes take flight,
In delicate dances, spirits unite.

Whispered secrets from the wind,
Tales of old, where worlds begin.
In quiet murmurs, life rescind,
A cosmic weave, so finely pinned.

Beneath the stars where dreams ignite,
Whispers mold the perfect sight.
Through the veil, past day and night,
Realities born, soft and bright.

Embrace the silence, breathe the air,
Whispered truths beyond compare.
In hidden depths, tender and rare,
Lies whispered dreams, beyond despair.

Journals of My Spirit

In pages worn, tales of old,
Stories of courage, gently unfold.
Words like whispers, bold and bold,
Journals of spirit, truths untold.

Across the ink, the past does trace,
A soul's journey, pace by pace.
Each passage holds a sacred space,
Where heart and spirit interlace.

In margins wide, dreams reside,
In letters' flow, the spirit's guide.
Through turns of time, emotions ride,
Journals bind what's deep inside.

Listen close, as echoes speak,
Through ancient lines, wisdom seek.
In humble scripts, whispers meek,
Strength and grace, so uniquely peak.

Journals filled with soul's delight,
In written shadows, dawns ignite.
Through time and space, life's insight,
Journals of spirit, pure and bright.

Heartfelt Scribbles

In hurried lines where feelings show,
A soul's whispers, ebb and flow.
Heartfelt scribbles, thoughts bestow,
Raw emotions, free to grow.

In scatterings of ink and pain,
Infinite joys, the sorrows wane.
Stories rendered in refrain,
Scribed in veins, a life's domain.

Unpolished gems, the words align,
Moments captured, raw, divine.
Heartfelt scribbles, line by line,
Reflective glimmers, stars that shine.

In margins wide or narrow scroll,
Hand's expression, spirit's role.
Each scribble bares a piece of soul,
Incomplete yet wholly whole.

In every dot and curved trace,
Love and truth find sacred space.
Heartfelt scribbles, life embrace,
Expressions pure, tender, grace.

Realm of Introspection

In shadows deep where echoes meet,
Introspections soft retreat.
Silent footsteps, whispered beat,
Thoughts unfold, discreet, complete.

Within the mind, the soul does weave,
Stories lived, beliefs conceive.
In realm of thought, truths retrieve,
From inner worlds, life perceive.

Quiet moments, reflections find,
Paths of heart and peace entwined.
Introspection, undefined,
Nurtures spirit, sharpens mind.

Echoes dance in silent halls,
Answers hidden, secret calls.
Introspection gently falls,
Wisdom's rise in humble thralls.

Inward gaze, a sacred quest,
Thoughts explored, the soul expressed.
In realm of silent, peaceful rest,
Introspection, life's behest.

Pages from My Core

In the silent drift of night, I find my pen,
To trace those whispers, echoes of the wind.
Thoughts unfurl as paper meets the ink,
Emotions surface, long buried deep within.

A dance of shadows, reflections of my soul,
Each line a heartbeat, a story to be told.
Some memories sweet, some etched in pain,
Yet all are precious, in this quiet domain.

Candles flicker, in my sacred space,
Guiding letters as they interlace.
A writer's haven, a sanctuary serene,
Where dreams spill out, unseen and clean.

The pages turn, with a gentle sigh,
Immortalizing moments that may not die.
Through studied strokes, my essence pours,
Into these pages, from my core.

The world outside, fades to a blur,
Here, thoughts and feelings gently stir.
Lost in the rhythm of paper and pen,
I breathe new life from within, again.

Musings from the Depths

In the quiet caverns of my mind,
Thoughts echo, twist and entwine.
Deeper still, where shadows play,
A well of musings, night and day.

Whispers of old awaken here,
Carrying secrets, joy and fear.
Voices of wisdom, ages old,
Stories of courage, yet untold.

Each reverie a canvas wide,
Breathing life, as dreams collide.
Splash of sorrow, tinge of bliss,
Painting worlds that coexist.

Beneath the surface, currents run,
Twining tales, yet begun.
These musings rise, from depths unfathomed,
Chiming truths, timeless and unpatterned.

With eyes closed, I venture deep,
To unearth the treasures I keep.
In these depths, I find the key,
To endless worlds, and all they see.

Diary of My Heart

Ink-stained pages, tender and worn,
Chronicle stories waiting to be adorned.
Each stroke a pulse, of life's steady play,
Guarding secrets, night and day.

Beneath the folds, where words reside,
Feelings breathed, no longer hide.
Joy and sorrow, interwoven tight,
A tapestry of heart, pure and bright.

Every tear and every grin,
Nestled softly, deep within.
Lines of hope, threads of despair,
Diary of my heart lays bare.

In this book, untouched by time,
Whispers of lore, in silent rhyme.
Pages bloom with every beat,
Echoing the love, incomplete.

Here I pen, each rise and fall,
Of moments grand and moments small.
This diary, a precious chart,
Mapping the voyage of my heart.

Emotional Odyssey

Set sail on waters, deep and blue,
With currents that drift, wild and true.
This odyssey through heart and thought,
Unveils the feelings long sought.

Through tempests fierce and calms so still,
Emotions rise, beyond my will.
Joy like sun on a bright dawn's crest,
Grief as storm clouds, manifest.

Love, a lighthouse on the shore,
Guiding when the waves implore.
Anchors of hope, hold me fast,
In this voyage, through the past.

Dreams like stars, in night's embrace,
Chart the course with gentle grace.
An endless sea of what could be,
Maps this emotional odyssey.

Each wave a whisper, tale, or plea,
Of hearts and minds that wander free.
To sail within, to seek and see,
Is the journey's true decree.

www.ingramcontent.com/pod-product-compliance
Lightning Source LLC
LaVergne TN
LVHW020450070526
838199LV00063B/4903